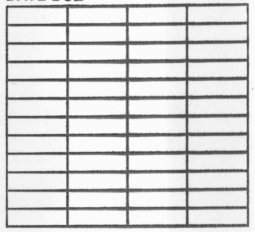

How Artists Use

Color

Paul Flux

Heinemann Library
Chicago, Illinois

Customer Service 888-454-2279

Visit our website at www.heinemannlibrary.com

Designed by Celia Floyd
Illustrations by Jo Brooker/Ann Miller
Originated by Ambassador Litho Ltd.
Printed and bound in Hong Kong/China

05 04 03 02 01
10 9 8 7 6 5 4 3 2 1

Library of Congress Cataloging-in-Publication Data
Flux, Paul, 1952-
        Color / Paul Flux.
                    p. cm.--(How artists use)
        Includes bibliographical references (p.) and index.
        ISBN 1-58810-078-2 (lib.bdg.)
        1. Color in art--Juvenile literature. 2. Color in art--Psychological aspects--Juvenile literature. 3. Painting--Technique--Juvenile literature. [1. Color. 2. Color in art. 3. Painting--Technique.] I. Title.

ND1492 .F58 2001
752--dc21

                                                                    00-058148

Acknowledgments
The Publishers would like to thank the following for permission to reproduce photographs:

© 2001 Mondrian/Holtzman Trust c/o Beeldrecht, Amsterdam, Holland & DACS, London, p. 20; AKG, London, pp. 7, 9, 14, 17, AKG, London/© ADAGP, Paris and DACS, London 2001, p. 27, AKG, London/© Munch Museum/Munch—Ellingsen Group, BONO, Oslo, DACS, London 2001, p.19; Boomalli Aboriginal Artists. Purchased with the assistance of funds from National Gallery admission charges and commissioned in 1987. Collection: National Gallery of Australia, Canberra, p.15; Bridgeman Art Library/© ADAGP, Paris and DACS pp16, 18, Bridgeman Art Library/© Kate Rothko Prizel and Christopher Rothko/DACS 2001, p. 12; Peter Willi, p. 11; Corbis/National Gallery, London, p. 28; SCALA, p. 10; Tate Gallery, London/© Succession H Matisse/DACS 2001, p. 13; Trevor Clifford/Jo Brooker, pp. 23, 24, 25.

Cover photograph reproduced with permission of Bridgeman Art Library.

Every effort has been made to contact copyright holders of any material reproduced in this book. Any omissions will be rectified in subsequent printings if notice is given to the Publisher.

Some words are in bold, **like this.** You can find out what they mean by looking in the glossary.

Contents

Making Colors

How many different colors do you think there are? Our eyes can see thousands of colors. Some of them are bright, and some are dark. Red, yellow, and blue are called **primary colors.** They cannot be made by mixing together other colors. Primary colors can be mixed to make every other color.

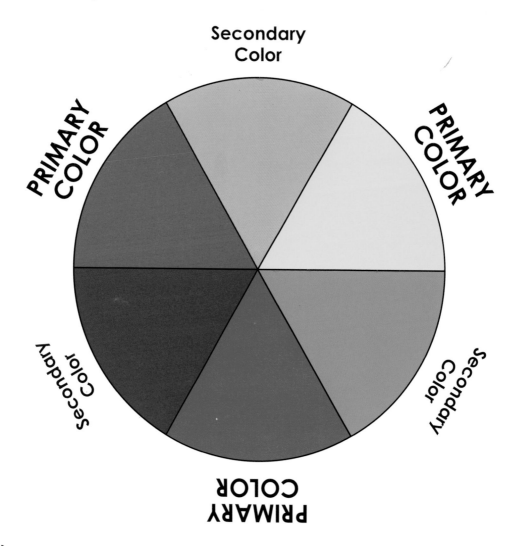

Secondary Color

PRIMARY COLOR

PRIMARY COLOR

Secondary Color

Secondary Color

PRIMARY COLOR

Secondary colors are made by mixing two primary colors together. By adding more of one color you get different **shades**. If you mix all three primary colors together you get a muddy brown.

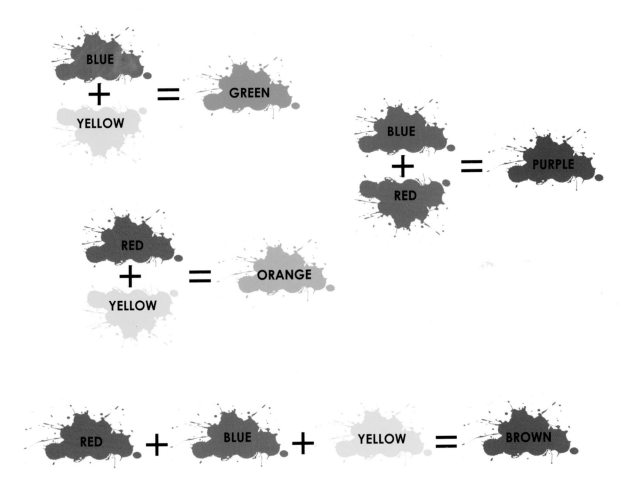

Color Partners

Opposite colors on the color wheel **complement** one another. This means that the colors work together so that they both stand out. Which red blob seems strongest to you? All three are exactly the same, but the one on the green background probably seems much brighter. The purple and orange blobs also seem very bright because they are with their **complementary color.**

Vincent van Gogh, *Portrait of the Postman Joseph Roulin,* 1889

Vincent van Gogh is well-known for his use of complementary colors. The green background in this painting **contrasts** with the dark hat and coat and the wavy beard to make the face of the postman really stand out. Likewise, the green eyes are strong and searching.

Warm and Cool Colors

Warm colors remind us of fire and sunshine. They are red, yellow, and orange. Often artists use these colors to show strong feelings, such as love or anger. Blue and green are cool colors. They may make us think of the sky and the ocean. When artists use cool colors their pictures can seem cold and lacking in feeling.

8

In this painting, the artist used warm colors to give the picture strength. He has placed fruit on a white cloth and surrounded it with **earth colors**. The warm colors bring the **scene** to life. They make the ordinary objects seem special. The colors make the apples look dazzling.

Paul Cézanne, *Apples and Oranges*, 1895–1900

Egyptian hieroglyphic writing

Color can add meaning to many types of art.
Look at these ancient Egyptian letters, which we call
hieroglyphs. The walls of the tombs of kings were often
covered with writing like this. The colors do not change
what the meaning is, but the yellows, greens, and browns
make the writing more **decorative**.

Rose window, Notre Dame Cathedral, Paris, about 1250

Stained glass is often found in churches and has been used for hundreds of years. This window was made more than 700 years ago. Light shines through the glass and fills the inside of the building with bright colors. People standing beneath this window can be covered with rainbow colors. The **shade** of each color changes as the light outside changes.

How Artists Use Color

Artists use color in many ways. This artist used big blocks of color with fuzzy edges to show different moods and feelings. This kind of art is called **abstract**. It focuses on color and shape.

Mark Rothko, *White Cloud over Purple,* **1957**

12

Henri Matisse made this picture when he was over 80 years old. His helpers painted large sheets of paper, and Matisse cut them into shapes and stuck them onto **canvas**. He wanted to **explore** the difference between drawing objects and using color to show them in art. After it was finished, Matisse called this picture *The Snail*.

Henri Matisse, *The Snail*, 1953

Color Adds Meaning

Fra Angelico, *The Annunciation*, 1437–1445

This painting is on the wall of a **monastery** in Florence, Italy. Look closely at the angel's wings. The blue and orange feathers **complement** one other, and so do the red clothes and green grass. Here color is being used to help express deep religious feelings.

14

Around 200 years ago, people from Europe discovered Australia and moved there. In 1988 many Australians celebrated this event. The **Aboriginal** people had mixed feelings about the celebration, because much of their land had been taken by the settlers. A group of 43 Aboriginal artists made this forest of poles. The **earth colors** and ancient **designs** of the 200 poles celebrate Aboriginal culture.

Ramingining Artists, *The Aboriginal Memorial,* **1987–1988**

Colors in Balance

The French artist Claude Monet was interested in the effect of light on everyday **scenes**. He often painted many pictures of the same place at different times of the day. In this beautiful painting he has balanced the blue light of early evening in winter with an orange sky. There is a sense of stillness in this painting. The colors **combine** to create a feeling of great peace.

Claude Monet, *Haystacks: Snow Effect,* 1891

16

Caspar David Friedrich, *The Monk by the Sea*, 1808–1810

Many paintings work well when the colors are used in
balance. Here we can see a cloudy sky reflected on
a bare cliff top. The blue and purple **tones** weave
together to create a feeling of enormous space. The
lone man gazing into the distance seems small set
against the huge sky.

Colors that Shout!

Joan Miró, *Figures in the Night*, 1960

Colors can be used in ways that surprise us. In this picture, dark night-time shapes are surrounded by strong splashes of color. These bright **tones** are held in check by the dark figures in front and the dark sky in back. The bright colors may mean excitement or danger. The dark figures might represent shadows.

Edvard Munch, *The Scream*, 1893

Bold colors are used here to give the painting a strong sense of feeling. Swirling **shades** of red and orange push out from the **canvas.** The bright colors **contrast** with the darkness on the side and add a feeling of fear or worry to the painting.

Color and the Modern World

The straight lines of New York City's streets gave the artist the idea for this **abstract** painting. The rigid lines are like city streets. The bright colors seem to indicate movement and excitement. Perhaps the colors are like the cars on the street or the theater signs above the sidewalk.

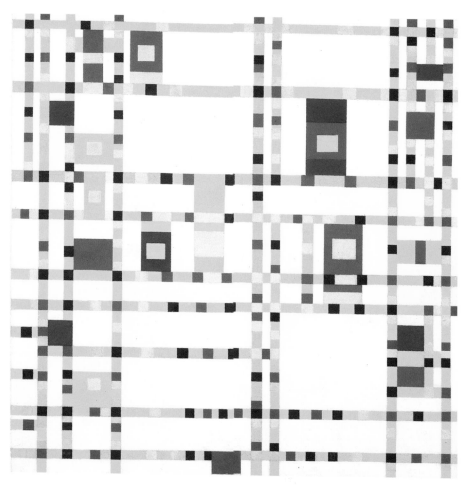

Piet Mondrian, *Broadway Boogie Woogie,* 1942–1943

Today we can use computers to make great pictures. Colors, lines, and shapes can all be changed very quickly, and patterns can be repeated easily. The bright colors of this computer-generated art may reflect the artist's excitement about these new ways to make art.

Mixing Colors

Start with one of the **primary colors** and **experiment** by adding different colors to it. Keep a record of which colors you have mixed and the new colors you make. Use the different **shades** you have made to paint something simple like the sky, water, or a field of grass.

Collect lots of colored see-through candy wrappers.
Tape some of the wrappers to a window and **overlap**
them to make different colors. Make as many
different colors as you can. If you want to make a
color stronger, fold the wrappers in half.

Spinning colors can have a strange effect. You can make some simple spinners and decorate them. Use the **designs** shown here to help you. What seems to happen to the colors as the paper spins? What happens when you use two **primary colors** together? What happens when you only use black and white?

How to make a spinner

1. Cut out a circle of posterboard 6 in. (15 cm.) wide. Ask an adult to make two holes about 1/3 in. (1 cm.) from the center.
2. Draw a design on one side and color it. Repeat the design on the other side, but color it differently.
3. Get some thin string or yarn and thread it through the two holes. Knot the string to make a loop.

Hold the string in both hands. Twist it, then gently pull. As the card spins you will see the colors change.

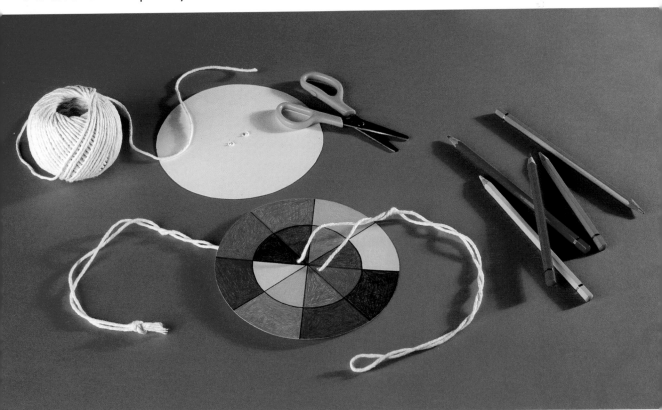

Colors and Tones

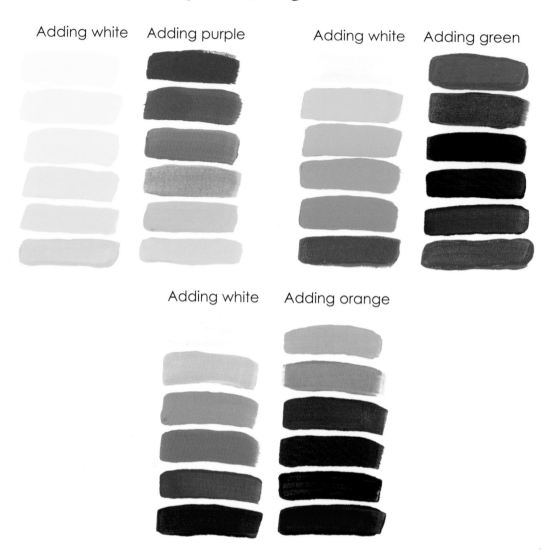

Adding white | Adding purple | Adding white | Adding green

Adding white | Adding orange

Put two big blobs of a **primary color** paint on a **palette**. Slowly add white paint to one of the blobs. Add tiny amounts of the **complementary color** to the other blob. As you discover different **shades**, make your own **tone** ladders like the ones above. Tones that line up with each other on the ladders often work best together.

Here the artist has used the light and dark tones of purple, blue, and green to paint a lily pond. The delicate coloring suggests that the time is early morning or evening. Monet was interested in the way light and water **interacted** to continually change the **scene**.

Claude Monet, *Water Lilies*, 1907

Painting with Dots

Georges Pierre Seurat, *Bathers at Asnières,* 1883–1884

This artist **experimented** with color in a **scientific** way.
He did not paint with **brush strokes**. Instead, he used
tiny dots of color. Look at the boy on the right side of
the picture. He seems surrounded with bright light.
The artist used light and dark **tones** and mixed them
together to create this special effect.

This way of painting tricks us into seeing many colors. The colors do not blend together on the **canvas,** but in our minds we see the blended colors. Try experimenting with tiny dots of color. Make a simple picture using only dots of color.

Glossary

Aboriginal native of Australia

abstract kind of art that does not try to show people or things, but instead focuses on shape and color

brush strokes marks in paint made by a brush

canvas strong woven material on which many artists paint

combine to mix two or more things together

complement to make another color seem bright

complementary colors colors opposite one another on the color wheel

contrast to show a noticeable difference

decorative pleasant or interesting to look at

design lines and shapes that decorate art

earth color warm color found in nature, such as brown or red

experiment to repeat something in different ways until you like the result

explore to examine how something works

hieroglyph symbol used by the ancient Egyptians in picture writing

interact how two or more things work together

monastery building where men called monks live and pray

overlap to partly cover

palette thin board or dish used to mix and holdcolors

primary colors red, blue, and yellow; colors that cannot be made by mixing other colors

secondary color color that is made by mixing two primary colors together

scene view painted by an artist or place where something happens

scientific testing ideas in an ordered way, as in science

shade darker or lighter version of a color

stained glass pieces of colored glass put together to make a picture

tone depth of color, from light to dark or dull to bright

More Books to Read

Richardson, Joy. *Using Color in Art*. Milwaukee, Wisc.: Gareth Stevens, 1996.

Riley, Peter D. *Light and Colors*. Danbury, Conn.: Watts, Franklin, 1999.

Index